EFFECTIVE VIDEO

How To Make Videos That Sell. Tips And Strategies

FIRST EDITION

Cover Illustration Copyright © 2019 by Teamcrea_tive

Editing by Tasha Joan Gagnon

Ebook ISBN: 978-1-7343113-1-0

Hardcover ISBN: 978-1-7343113-0-3

Published By Engaging New Media, LLC

www.engagingnewmedia.com

TABLE OF CONTENTS

INTRODUCTION

Visual marketing is gold!

T he world, as we know it, is visual. Most of the content around us can only be filtered through our eyes and, as such, they inform our decisions, temper our reactions, and, of course, influence our behavioral patterns. Whether in brochures, on websites, or one-on-one, visual content (also the most effective solution) appeals to the psyche, and indeed, grabs the consumer's attention. Notably, several marketing books out there promise significant business turnover if the methods are accurately applied. Honestly, many of these written books live up to standard. Few, unfortunately, highlight the relationship between marketing and design. Pointedly, while marketing influences the behavior of consumers, design informs the visuals.

There's never been a better time in history for online businesses to explore video marketing strategies and other forms of three-dimensional visuals. The advent of technology shows that small businesses and online businesses can incorporate visuals into their methodology—visuals that were only available to big corporations with the right tools to make it happen. Thankfully, the internet offers convenience, in terms

1

of finding and hiring the best design professionals to impact successful marketing goals. And if you buy into the DIY lifestyle, there are many design tools and software services that you can experiment with by creating visual content from the comfort of your home.

CHAPTER 1

WHAT IS VISUAL STORYTELLING?

When you use images, especially videos, presentations, and infographics, on social media channels, you create graphical stories for your brand or online business. You've probably heard how other online business owners and marketers chant the 'content is king' slogan, but the introduction of social media platforms, such as Instagram, Pinterest, and even Facebook, has ushered in the popular adage 'a picture speaks a thousand words.' 21st century marketers are increasing their social media engagement with visuals—video marketing, especially. But you must know that your online business won't survive on posting videos and images alone. As a company, you should embrace visual storytelling by creating quality content and sharing it with the target audience. It is not surprising that these companies are the leaders of the pack when it comes to optimum engagement, sales, and referral traffic.

The rise of visual social media marketing has also resulted in the present economy, where the consumers react to visual content better than ordinary, text-filled content. For instance, on Pinterest boards, you can plan your meals with shared images and videos and organize your wardrobe from the safety of your home. Visual content and storytelling keep getting better with each passing hour. Contrary to text-prone content, visual storytelling is a strategy that adopts the 'show, don't tell' technique to achieve:

- ❖ Engagement

- ❖ Conversation and conversion

- ❖ Sharing

80 percent of active internet users in the United States of America are estimated to adopt blogs and social media, setting the gold standard as action and engagement. Try this straightforward experiment—post content with an album or video on your Instagram and watch how you get about 180 percent engagement from your followers, compared to essential text-filled content. Instagram users post millions of photos and videos every day with thousands of likes and comments per second. Artists, especially, do not fail to leverage their YouTube channels upon the release of a video and the most promising of them receive an average of 20 million views after a while.

Visual storytelling is helping millions of people to prioritize and act; whether it's watching a YouTube video that propels action or using Pinterest to find new hacks in the kitchen.

Let's look at Sephora. The company stated that its followers on Pinterest spend fifteen times more than those on Facebook. The company has more than 18 million followers on Instagram and more than 200,000 on Pinterest with prominent boards like 'Nailspotting,' 'Travel,' and more. Sephora's Pinterest, like many other accounts, has a 'Most Popular Pins' board which shares the most converted (generating thousands of likes and shares) pins. Like Sephora, Calgary Zoo also generated interest and headlined national news when it launched its Instagram in place of a traditional PDF. Its 2012 annual report, tagged ``The Year of the Penguins," featured report pages and content as numerous photos (with captions), telling the story of the zoo's accomplishments since inception in a uniquely fascinating visual fashion. Heard of Blendtec? The visual storytelling revolution started when the brand launched its 'Will it blend?' series. After watching an R&D video where wooden boards were blended, Blendtec's marketing team invested about $100 in some 'wacky' supplies and shared videos on their YouTube channel with the caption 'Will it Blend?' Some consumers' favorite was the peculiar video clip showing the latest iPhone being blended into tiny bits.

Visual storytelling has evolved

Do you belong to the bandwagon of people that believe visual storytelling is an overnight sensation? Well, you'll be shocked to know that visual storytelling has always been around, but the constant evolution of social media channels and consumer behaviors ultimately influenced the patterns. During the late '90s, popular blogging platforms—Flickr, Myspace, and Facebook—affected the use of visual engagement, thereby creating opportunities for budding bloggers. A closer look at the platforms showed that they were created in response to the influx of content on the web space, tons of which were either photos or videos. Back then, too, visual blog posts performed better than their text-based counterparts. The photo-sharing platform, Flickr, was quite the sensation in the early 2000s and still maintains a population of professional photographers and enthusiasts alike. Myspace also offered its users the singular opportunity to personalize content, music, and profiles. Besides the type of content, these social media giants had the extraordinary ability to pool like-minded crowds on the internet. Like today, when there are numerous social media platforms for customer engagement, like-minded users and consumers always discovered online communities with shared interests.

The key, it seems, was to identify the need of the consumer, what would bring them online, the possible values to be derived, and how you could fit within the engagement metrics. Apart from community engagement, the platforms' activities affirmed that the users needed new ways to organize and share content, videos, and imagery. From curating branded Myspace profiles complete with music videos to revering favorite bloggers on LiveJournal, and using Flickr to build photo albums, the truth of the saying 'Content is King' is truly confirmed and it's here to stay, perhaps for eternity. The hook for inspiring engagement and action across all social media channels has always been content, but the rules evolved, as did the social media channels. The layout of Facebook, for instance, between 2013 and 2019 offers a new window to witness the fascinating changes that are taking place on every social media platform. 2016 marked the year when Instagram increased its 15-second video limit to a 60-second window, coupled with the introduction of multiple slides so that online businesses could leverage visual storytelling to their advantage. Some months later, the introduction of Live Story, an interface for sharing real-time content with your followers on Instagram, followed.

Back on Facebook, the formerly text-heavy platform allowed group pages and user profiles and upon acquiring Instagram, interlaced its platform with the 'News Feed' and 'Story' features for sharing vibrant videos and photos. Like Instagram, Facebook users began to yearn for a platform on which they could scroll through multiple layouts to find their favorite items or content. The constant increase in the number of mobile Facebook users showed, also, that consumers are always in search of a seamless experience on every device. In 2004, when Facebook first launched the platform, what could be seen was a directory of contact information, interests, and usernames. You had to navigate a selected profile to abstract user information. Coupled with the text-heavy layout, the user's profile photo was the most prominent image. By joining groups nowadays, Facebook offers a chance to share your interests, foster engagement, and cultivate an identity. The 'News Feed' feature, accompanied by Mini-Feed came into existence in 2006; it was largely visible on the home page and it offered a cute collection of information from different friends, groups, tags, and activities. The mini-feed, on the other hand, offered updates on a friend's Facebook profile and subsequent changes. Rather quickly, users began to enjoy the sweet trend of viewing friends' statuses, including attached photos and videos. This user experience formed the basis of the 'News Feed Layout' in the present Facebook. From 2007 to 2012, Facebook evolved into a more visual interface, creating opportunities for video marketers to tap into the stream of income offered by the platform. Back then and now, you would 'like' a favorite company's or public figure's Facebook profile as an indication of fanatism. In 2007, Facebook had to filter about 30,000 story updates on News Feed into a customized stream of 60 stories for the everyday use of each user. This meant that every News Feed with text placements could be equated to being on Google's first search result page. The text placements package, which was premium, was out of reach for many online businesses and brands because they couldn't pay the fees, develop an app, or insert ads into their News Feed. One year later, new apps (such as WhatsApp) made sure to include status updates so that consumers could share images, videos, and content within groups and pages. Yet, the content was distributed through update notifications or inbox messages. Users had to have the willpower to click and proceed to the page or group on which the content had been shared, meaning that the content had to work harder to gain engagement. The launch of Facebook Timeline took everyone by storm, as users could 'tell their stories' with simple videos, images, and content, making available an interactive platform, in contrast to the previously text-heavy interface. Facebook users had at their disposal a digital and shareable layout with options for the cover photo and broader tabs to fill in historical information.

For brands, Timeline ensured that brand owners enjoyed similar benefits by promoting visual content dynamically and phenomenally and the results were shocking. A few days after the introduction of Facebook Timeline, videos and photos (visual content) had a more than 60 percent increase in customer engagement. Facebook announced an update to the News Feed in 2013. According to CEO Mark Zuckerberg, at the press conference, the evolution in content sharing on social media precipitated the needed update in the News Feed. The critical changes were focused mainly on images, access to multiple feeds, and mobile optimization. More than half of the population of active users on Facebook (1 billion) in 2012 had adopted Facebook's mobile products. Facebook also confirmed that the latest updates showed praiseworthy activity, scoring 50 percent improvement over the previous text-heavy interface. Now, Facebook engagement debunks the early rules that companies stacked experience from prominent brands, gravitating towards the promotion of interactions in News Feed. Users now use the platform to share travel content, catch up with friends, and seek out information. This behavior cuts across several social media platforms, except for Pinterest, whose principal focus is on categorizing and sharing visual content. Although challenging to brands and business owners, many users do not like being interrupted by brand-generated content and ads on their news feed. Therefore, brands must work harder to be a 'delectable interruption' by having 'attention-grabbing,' 'strong affinity,' and 'prompt action' qualities to stay relevant and avoid being 'unliked' by such users. On Facebook too, users can always hide unwanted promotions or content on News Feed, a choice that is worse than an unlike as brands do not have a fair measure of their activities or general acceptance by many users, who have probably hidden their content from their News Feed. The introduction of a Facebook algorithm called EdgeRank, alongside the current changes, which help to determine which posts will appear on your News Feed and where they will appear, have emphasized the significance of visual storytelling and engagement in the digital world. Since the News Feed marks the most appealing site engagement, videos, and images catch the attention of other users than mere texts, pulling more engagement for the user. By inference, posts made by brands and companies will make it to the News Feed of fans if the present users are positively engaged in the posts. Sharing and engagement thrives since fans can infiltrate new audiences, using the friend of friend feature, prompting increased engagement and subsequent fan growth. EdgeRank conditions thriving brands and online businesses to avoid 'resting on their oars.' Content must be churned out with a few things in mind—weight, affinity, and timing. The content is ranked based on the frequency of engagement, the sentiment of interaction, and of course, volume, and other Facebook users can easily find such content if they are high ranked. In those years, brands often criticized Facebook for the algorithm, which chooses 'any' content, not minding the amount of hard work the marketers have put into growing their Facebook fan base, releasing the content to a tiny percentage of that fan base.

CHAPTER 2

VISUAL STORYTELLING

VIDEO MARKETING FOR YOUR

ONLINE BUSINESS

Videos are a vibrant and stimulating aspect of storytelling in business. Not only do viewers appreciate what they can see the most, but they also have the means to engage with the advertised content. The continuous improvement and increased availability of bandwidth in video technology translate to an accelerated watch-time and sharing ratio for content. Funny clips, music videos, commercials, movie trailers, and animal reviews have created an exciting, educative, and informative avenue for consumers. In 2016 Hubspot listed popular video content according to the following percentages—comedy (39 percent), news (33 percent), and music (31 percent). More so, Google was ranked in September 2017 as the largest desktop search engine in the world, boasting of more than 90 percent of the global market share. YouTube followed with approximately 1 billion unique users, becoming the second largest search engine tube and the third most visited website in the world. By extension, more YouTube users are emerging, and they aren't merely browsing or expecting links to drop in their emails. Since more users are exposed to the trending video marketing tips, it has become a part of the world's digital strategy and there is a greater need to understand the creation and optimization of videos for online businesses.

Every day, YouTube users spend 1 billion hours watching videos online and more than half of the population accesses YouTube through their mobile devices. Meanwhile, users upload 400 hours of video every 60 seconds. As mentioned earlier, more social media sites are following the video trend. Expectedly, the end of 2006 witnessed a new turn in Facebook metrics when about 4 billion video views were recorded in a 24-hour cycle. Indeed, Facebook videos can reach ten times more people than shared YouTube links. Further, the introduction of Periscope and Facebook Live—live video platforms—allows users to spend three times longer in watching videos than prerecorded types. Indeed, no one truly knows the sources of these videos as they could come from anywhere. The famous 'Charlie Bit My Finger' video showed that small videos might experience an unpredictable global reach, as the video amassed 800+ million views in 2017.

Likewise, more brands are tapping into the video-sharing field to make stronger and impactful connections with prospective and existing customers, boosting the strength of their brands by creating responses, parodies, and opinion videos. Now, business owners can market their ideas, offers, and brand promise. As seen, video content fosters a stronger connection with consumers by creating an excellent user experience and encouraging customer engagement.

Basic terms and concepts in video marketing

- ❖ Annotation – These are instructions or comments which are added as text, especially on YouTube videos. For instance, a YouTube annotation may feature action-driven links that direct users to further pages—within YouTube or an external site. In 2017, annotations were replaced with video cards.

- ❖ Captions – Captions are texts that are infused into video scenes. You see them over videos either narrating dialogues on the screen or identifying a particular person or location. However, there are open captions and closed captions.

- ❖ Embedding – The integration of links, images, videos, GIFs, and other content into social media posts, webpages, or other forms of web-based media.

- ❖ Google AdWords – Google Ads are search advertising programs provided by Google to allow respective advertisers to market their products or services on relevant search results and across all Google's algorithms.

❖ Metadata – This is a type of information that is entered about web pages and other elements to provide information to search engines.

❖ Search Engine Results Page (SERP) – This page features the results of the user's search query.

❖ Thumbnail – At the start of videos, thumbnails are featured as small and still images. When selected, they display the full content of the video and create an enticing video experience.

❖ Video cards – These calls to action often show up during a video and entice the viewers to perform specific actions. These are better replacements for annotations.

❖ Video Search Engine Optimization (VSEO) – Similar to how one would optimize websites to rank higher on Google, you can optimize videos for search engines.

❖ Video syndication – You can get better search coverage for uploaded videos when you distribute videos.

- ❖ Views – These refer to the frequency at which a video is watched or seen. A user may see a video multiple times.

- ❖ Viral video – An extremely popular video, either because of the number of views and shares it has gained or through word of mouth across the web, hosting websites, social networks, or email.

- ❖ Vlogger – Also known as a 'video blogger.' Refers to an individual that produces many web videos about selected topics and content and shares it on a video-enabled blog.

Reasons to use video marketing in your online business

Many infographics show how videos will influence online businesses in the near future. The power of videos means that the future is already here. Marketers are consistently tapping into the goldmine, and it calls for a complete revolution. Wyzowl, an animated explainer video company, people new to the industry may think the name is a typo, statistics show that video content marketing strategies cut across about 70 percent of businesses in the present day. 82 percent of that number believes that video marketing is the secret ingredient to their business success and total business strategy. This consensus and more are influencing the rapid progress of businesses, and soon, videos will attain new heights in the globe. The trend is completely backed up by 83 percent of users who have proven that video marketing is responsible for their excellent ROI.

Without a doubt, the latest addition to the promotion arsenal is video marketing. While there may be a few doubting Thomases out there, promoting your business with videos is worth your consideration for many reasons. And a simple question to ponder is: does video marketing exhibit promotional potentials for your business? If yes, do you have the needed resources to pursue video marketing in your online business?

Video marketing is an irrefutable boon. Not only because every Tom, Dick, and Harry follows the trend, but because it is a profitable and versatile venture for digital marketing enthusiasts.

1. Videos drive conversions and sales

Probably everyone knows now that videos can generate significant revenue. Every time you add a video to a product on your landing page, you boost the chances of that product selling by 80 percent. Regardless of the video category, you can be confident that the product conversion will be massive. Similarly, videos affect the direct sales of products. Recently, another survey showed that 74 percent of users, after watching a brief video about a product or service, bought that product or service. Why, then, would you refuse an efficient video marketing strategy?

Let's think about it. The effect of videos on sales and conversion is certainly not surprising. We know that our vision, more than other senses of perception, is most dominant. Our brain is entirely capable of processing visual images. Now, if pictures boost business success already, you can imagine the effect of moving pictures on the business.

2. Businesses witness high ROI with videos

Let's get more excited. More than 80 percent of businesses yield a high return on investment (ROI). Although video production is quite an expensive venture, the anticipated benefits and profits are worth the try. Even as online video editing tools keep emerging and improving, you can expect better affordability of these services, even when you contact professional video marketers. Let's not forget that our smartphones are capable of stringing together creative and decent videos to propel newly started or tightly budgeted business. Great news! Your video doesn't even have to be near-perfect in the beginning, before you can publish and share them. What matters the most is the content of the video. Another study proves that users are entirely turned off by videos that don't offer concise explanations for products and services. It simply shows how important it is to invest in a professional video marketing service for targeted results.

3. Videos build customer trust

The foundation of sales and conversions is trust. Hence, you should strive to build trust with your consumers by putting out good videos. Content marketing itself is carefully built on trust and the creation of long-term relationships. Don't focus intently on selling. Instead, churn out useful and interesting information for the consumer's use. The Executive Director of Schaefer Marketing Solutions mentioned that a new era of marketing demands less content and more ignition, less traffic and more trust, and people in the loop who steadily spread and advocate your content.

Videos are all-encompassing. When you upload a video, you ignite the emotions of the consumers as much as you engage the audience. And when it comes down to elite consumers, YouTubers (vloggers) are often the most powerful people that can promote your business. Thus, you must take video marketing as seriously as content marketing.

You can also foster trust with promotional videos. Some consumers have admitted that they are always skeptical about making purchases due to fear of being defrauded or cheated by the seller. After all, in an era where you get to pay for a product or service before delivery, extra care is needed in identifying legitimate sellers. Compelling marketing videos can present your products interactively. This sense of individual approach is the reason that 50 percent of consumers admit that videos drive confident purchases.

4.   Google is a fan of videos

When you share your videos, consumers spend more time on your page or website. More prolonged exposure builds trust and signals prominent search engines that your brand represents excellent content. Moovly says that if there is a video on your page, you are 53 times more likely to be listed on Google search pages. Since Google acquired YouTube, the rate at which videos places you on search engine pages increases.

You can adopt SEO strategies by optimizing videos on sites such as YouTube. Start by writing fascinating descriptions and titles for the product or service. Then, you may add a link that directs users to your website to purchase your products or services. This is a perfect call to action that helps the consumer take further steps. To encourage your target audience, you shouldn't forget to explore several interactive video options.

5.   Mobile users prefer video content

About 90 percent of mobile users spend a lot of time on their phones exploring videos. The third quarter in 2013 saw a rise in mobile video views, earning an increase of more than 233 percent over time. Also, YouTube showed 100 percent in video consumption annually. Since people are generally fans of a good watch, smartphone users are increasing in high numbers, and the video audience rises in response. Google shows that smartphone users are 1.4 times more likely as desktop viewers and two times more likely than TV audiences to gravitate towards brands that share video ads and content.

As mobile videos grow, it means that brands must pay attention to the personal user experience that people gain on smartphones. For instance, provide a better choice in video content consumed by your audience.

6. Video marketing explains the product or service at a glance and with a few words

If you are launching a new product or service, you should create an exciting video that shows 'how-to'. An explainer video, for instance, can influence buying power and 98 percent of users approve of this. Now, 45 percent of businesses feature explainer videos on their sites to drive engagement. 83 percent of those businesses proved that the explainer videos were quite useful.

Need to explain a difficult concept? Animated videos are the way to go. Animations break down concepts better than live videos or texts. Besides, many minutes of watching boring people explain an intricate concept can be draining. But with animations, you can blend nostalgia, entertainment, and simplicity in one video. The foremost goal should be the adoption of an active process. Nevertheless, there are a few pre-production steps which can uniquely position your video among hundreds of others.

7. Video engages every type of buyer

While videos are simple tools for learning, the laziest buyers attest that they are also straightforward to consume. Our lives, today, have shifted from reading text-heavy product descriptions before making purchases, when you can watch a 15-second video and get more information on-the-go. Every customer seeks value for purchases made, meaning that it is quite preferable to see the product in action. In that case, you may adopt video preference in your content marketing strategy.

Video marketing captures a broader audience, as can be seen nowadays, since it ensnares lazy buyers. Thus, you may want to target both the eyes and the ears of the potential buyers. This gives you a competitive advantage and indeed, doubles power over competitors.

8. Video fuels social shares

Michael Stelzner, at the 8th annual Social Media Marketing

Industry Report, mentioned that more than half of the population of social marketers had reliable video marketing strategies in 2015 and an estimated 73 percent of the respondents launched the same strategy in the following year.

We will remember that social media channels are sporadically infusing video platforms too. Facebook, for instance, launched Lifestage (for teenagers), Live Video, and 360 Video. Meanwhile, Instagram launched Instagram Stories, and 60-second videos on their platform, and Periscope on Twitter is not left out. Not forgetting YouTube, the second most popular social network is also making waves.

In a social media context, video marketers care to include more emotions than facts in their campaigns. As such, 76 percent of users often shared a video with their friends if it proved entertaining. Thus, the rational way to gain social shares is to create engaging videos on your site. Indeed, emotions do not necessarily translate to ROI, but social shares influence traffic and, by extension, affect ROI.

Bonus Tip—Video ads are miraculous

When you put up a video ad, its average click-through rate (CTR), as long as you adopt reliable marketing strategies in combination, is 1.84 percent. Across all digital ad formats, this CTR is the highest. The completion rate of a 15-second nonskippable YouTube video is slightly higher at 92 percent, and a skippable video ad rate is 9 percent.

Video ads mostly thrive on social media platforms, namely Facebook. Facebook, with Nielsen, described the value of video ads, stating that 74 percent of total Ad Recall is possible within a 10-second window frame. Thus, video ads make better substitutes than banners.

Bonus tip 2—Video is making waves in email campaigns

To make email marketing campaigns more interesting, you might want to incorporate exciting videos. Introductory emails with video attachments pull more than 90 percent CTR. And that type of percentage is a great way to stand out from the pack.

Top video trends in 2018

1. More consumers will watch videos ten times before reading the content. In content marketing, the video explosion is hugely influenced by consumer preference. Videos influence, generating and converting leads. You should know that potential buyers ignore many salespeople. Hence, the video will make up for customer conversion. The increased popularity of videos shows that video and content should go hand in hand.

2. The quality of content is essential, just as much as the

production quality. Technical aspects and production quality do not have to be topnotch. Better production quality cannot make up for lack of substance, although it improves trust between the customer and business owner. Thus, webinar recordings, Live Videos, and other video materials are substantial, with the condition that the content is engaging.

3 The acceptance of basic video production types will increase the use of ad-hoc video creation apps such as Instagram, Facebook, and Twitter.

4 As such, brands will start infusing video marketing into their business. Most brands will be concerned with getting mileage from their videos since different channels and video formats can work in consonance.

5 Visual storytelling is perhaps the most effective strategy nowadays. People may skim through a few instructions in an article, but a bad presentation can affect your audience's responses. The emotional connection and presentation technique of the script to the viewer can either make or mar your video.

6 Promotional testing. A lot of experiments need to go into finding the best approach to video. There's no rule that says you have to do things a certain way.

7   You have to optimize videos for specific platforms and different uses. For instance, you may upload videos without sound and synchronize video with on-screen text and subtitles. Some research proves that on-screen language subtitles influence better message recall.

8   Live video streams are an essential aspect of video content. You build brand awareness and engagement when you bring live events to audiences, interviews with influencers, and live sessions.

9   Video equals YouTube. YouTube serves as a template, even to big companies like Facebook. As the face of video leadership, YouTube offers an independent platform for vloggers and content creators to build their brand, business owners alike. Monetization is one of the strong points of YouTube, not Facebook. It is why Facebook strives to bring some YouTube stars to the platform.

10 Videos are used in personal sales and support. Brands go about this in two ways—record short messages for primary consumer needs, so that they can watch them whenever convenient and adopt pre-recorded clips with a support team.

11 Video marketing has an attractive ROI. It may be hard to measure excellent video content, but releasing more videos helps the sales process and improves conversion. Videos can boost sales if the prospects pick up speed.

Video advertising is the real gold in the present day. As it becomes more widespread, it also becomes more affordable with time. The adoption of videos is quite natural because of the advancement in technology and partly because videos are innately viral entities. Your business will appreciate marketing videos if you infuse your creativity and some human psychology. The cocktail of these elements means that you can create an extraordinary miracle of cheap advertising.

In a matter of days, you can spread a creative and emotionally charged video ad and get thousands, even millions, of views after some time. Therein lies the crux of video marketing—the creative survives.

CHAPTER 3

HOW VIDEO MARKETING WORKS IN THE REAL WORLD

If you run an online business, you must tap into the wealth of opportunities that abound on the internet and video marketing comes as the most recommended of all. Apart from the number of people that watch online videos, the reasons why these people watch the videos is of utmost importance. Posting a marketing video on your social media channel or website only means that more people can engage with your product or service. But you may want to know why video marketing is particularly essential for your business. Yes, video marketing creates several opportunities for business growth.

❖ An average American owns about four digital services and the same individual spends approximately 60 hours a week consuming online content

❖ More than 50 percent watch a video from start to finish in less than 60 seconds

❖ An internet user will spend about 90 percent of their time on a video site

As more consumers in the United States are trying to take advantage of convenience shopping, since tablets and smartphones create a vast opportunity for the marketability of brands. Are your consumers or target audience in different places? Videos foster an immediate bond between consumers anytime and anywhere. When you are asleep, and your staff are unable to attend to queries, an informative and entertaining video will fill in the blanks. Therefore, your video must have the qualities of emotional engagement, lest you risk losing potential customers and influencers.

- ❖ Appealing videos stand the test of time
- ❖ People like amusing and outrageous videos
- ❖ People love good humor

In the e-commerce industry, you will see product video catalogues, and these are strategic videos that boost the rate at which customers add items to their baskets and proceed to checkout. There are several types of videos and more than a hundred types of video production. They can be as expensive and sophisticated as producing professional video campaigns for the Super Bowl or as basic as using a smartphone. A good video must be consistent with the business objectives. Thus, ensure that you understand video marketing metrics. Highlight your goals and benchmark video marketing throughout the campaign.

What are your business needs?

- ❖ Do you want to develop a strategic search engine optimization technique?

- ❖ Increase brand awareness?

- ❖ Are you struggling with customer engagement?

- ❖ Need a faster way to reach both potential and existing customers?

- ❖ How do you intend to communicate your brand story?

- ❖ Identify your target audience

- ❖ Determine what your target audience cares about

- ❖ Do you have a meaningful concept that can be made into a video?

- ❖ How many videos will work in line with achieving your goals?

- ❖ What style of content can you adopt for your communication goals?

The types of video you choose are determined by the message you are trying to convey. Different purposes birth different genres of videos. It means that you must understand your audience's needs before you launch a creative process, and you must address the missing links in your existing content. Are your target customers in need of demo videos or 'how-to' commercials? Do you need customer testimonials? Is your company in need of an image video?

Most importantly, conduct qualitative research on competitors and find out what they are doing for their audience that makes them so indispensable. Necessarily, you may be wrong to choose what resonates with your audience if you don't try to understand them first. If done correctly, a creative and well-crafted message makes up for the budget deficit. If you already have a team, write a script as a team, since your employees will be your first experiment.

Steps to consider before working on a video concept

- ❖ Streamline the focus and topic

- ❖ Recruit a professional video marketer consultant

- ❖ Iterate your content for the next few months (preferably 6 to 12 months)

- ❖ Build a sustainable strategy

- ❖ Repurpose your video—consider the technical requirements of all platforms including your website and other social media channels

Although marketers are adopting videos to drive business success, that alone will not suffice. In your business, you must have a cohesive strategy that includes every type of relevant content and getting the most out of the video requires that you share it methodically.

The elements of video marketing

Like how friends nurture their relationship, video marketing offers online businesses a unique chance to impact positivity, which builds trust, brand awareness, and engaged communities. The key to developing and implementing a successful video marketing strategy is in the following elements—design, personalization, usefulness, personality, storytelling, share worthiness, and real-time amplification.

1 Visual imagery

The design element of visual marketing cuts across many industries and companies, some exceptional and the rest merely striving. Talented artists and photographers are hard to find these days, for sure.

Personalize always

Video marketing explores content personalization on every platform. Those days when you could spray the same content over myriads of platforms are gone. Instead, use the special features of each social media platform to foster storytelling and engagement. General Electric is a perfect example of a brand that continually adopts one-of-a-kind strategies for video marketing across several platforms. Whether you are on YouTube, Instagram, Facebook, or Pinterest, content is not continuous, but consistent across science and innovation themes. One of the unique approaches of the brand, General Electric, is widely varied on Pinterest, which showcases several boards. Since the goal of the company is to inspire power, the board titles as expected are "Mind=Blown", "Badass Machines", "GEInspiredMe", and more. You will also find a humorous "Hey Girl" board, which features crisp Thomas Edison-inspired pick-up lines.

2 Make yourself useful

Online businesses are doing the most by leveraging the strength of every social media platform to stay relevant. Unfortunately, you will need more than 'personalization' to brag about useful content. Social listening will help companies remain relevant by uncovering trends and key themes for creating visual content. Social listening also bridges the gap between companies and consumers by helping the former understand what drives consumers and prompts several actions—engaging, sharing, or purchasing.

Whole Foods is a company that tries to meet and exceed the expectations of its consumers by always churning out useful content. The company alone has more than 500 social media accounts across local and national store levels. Local stores develop content about the latest offerings, latest happenings, and handles visuals across Instagram, Pinterest, and Facebook. The national level consumes the benefits of Pinterest. By the way, most people will likely not expect a grocery store to offer value with mere recipe content. However, the brand has become a Pinterest leader because of its ability to co-create.

Natanya Anderson, the director of social media at Whole Foods, shared some fun facts about the company during the Visual Voice panel at SXSW 2013. Anderson leaked a company strategy that Whole Foods would, for every pin, repin five things from followers and accredit the content to the right source.

In the aspect of co-creation, Whole Foods brings experts of different subject matter to pin relevant content. As a result of that, Pinterest generates traffic to recipes on the company website through the other social media channels of the brand. Anderson also mentioned that as of 2015, the then 110,000 Pinterest followers would generate 15 times more value than Twitter and Facebook combined. For instance, spaghetti squash, a popular recipe on Pinterest, was repined about 70,000 times, thus driving up to 50,000 views to the recipe on the brand's website.

3 Be Human, as much as possible

Video marketing, apart from being utterly useful, performs better when you infuse the human element. Being human is more about being a friend than a mere corporate entity. A friend possesses a personality, shares experiences, values the friendship, and understands there is a time for play and time to be serious. Being human means you won't put up a video that merely states 'buy this now.' Instead of hitting the nail on the head (going straight for the sale), you might want to think about how an individual will analyze and recommend your product to people in their circle. You also want to evaluate and learn the ways of popular influencers, who are in the habit of producing marketable content about their brands. In research, you will discover that trust comes, not only from their strong reputation but also from the way they share product packages.

You should reach for the gold, take a break from what people have to say about your company, and understand their other concerns. Learn what interests and causes make them tick and try to discover their motivations. For example, your customer base might be passionate about fashion or entertainment. So, you may craft content around fashion shows, runways, fabrics, and more. This is a strategic move because consumers aren't hopping on their gadgets to get the news from a company. Instead, they are going online to repost birthday pictures and vacation photos.

Another concept of being human is 'fitting in.' Thus, your goal should be in creating visual content that can be considered a 'pleasurable interruption' between updates, notifications, and content. A perfect way to expose your human side is to promote the sharing of user-generated content within your community. In #TheSweatLife campaign by Lululemon, the company encouraged fans to share, on social media, how they achieved their sweat life for an opportunity to be featured on Lululemon's social media channels. By using 'Olapic' service, the software that collects user-generated photos across Twitter, Instagram, and Facebook, the brand had access to shared content. Naturally, the strategy places Lululemon in the spotlight, and it did so by personalizing the brand so that fans and followers could live in the moment. Lululemon could create an inspiring video but engaging real people who wore their apparel in their videos was the exceptional promotional technique the brand needed at that time. Apart from being relatable, the strategy had people watching how clothing fit on fellow buyers and consumers, instead of regular models. They further used the images and videos to source fitness tips and styling ideas. According to Nancy Richardson, the Vice President of Lululemon's digital and brand strategy department, the campaign garnered more than 2 million views and 26,000 had participated in the challenge between launching in the fall of 2012 and spring of 2013.

4   Tell A Story

So far, the visual marketing examples are proof that unique visual marketing strategy requires that the use of visuals is as important as the storytelling element of the content. Stories come from different places; whether it's vital milestones, company values, how consumers enjoy products or services or staying relevant. For instance, the Daily Twist campaign by Oreo was a celebration of the company's hundredth birthday, where it developed about a hundred compelling pop culture-inspired images. Timely occasions and holidays celebrated in style were the Mars Rover landing, Hispanic Heritage Month, and National Talk like a Pirate Day. Even though each piece of content differed, the creativity in showcasing holidays and pop culture happenings for a specified time was the necessary 'storytelling' element. The campaign won accolades and awards because it redefined business-consumer relationships on another level.

5   Be shareworthy in everything

Like lightning in a bottle, brands and businesses are looking for seamless visual storytelling opportunities to strike a chord with consumers. Coca-Cola says the way to do that is by remaining 'shareworthy'. The SVP of integrated marketing communications and capabilities at Coca-Cola, Wendy Clark, told Fortune that each Facebook fan, out of more than a billion fans, was only a friend away from the entire Coca-Cola community. Thus, strategic visual content in business would make the fans become the brand's sales force at no cost. Clark further stated that many brands should consider the customers as personal storytellers if they could imbibe the principle of initial and ultimate audiences by thinking about consumers as storytellers, rather than usual receivers of content. The SVP further mentioned that 80 percent of conversations about the brand was from consumers, and this action opened a window of co-creation instead of continually putting out content.

An exemplary storytelling act by Coca-Cola was the #BestSummerMoment campaign that was hosted across the company's social media channels and a microsite which prompted users to share their memorable summer moments. Coca-Cola celebrated these fans by sharing some of their content on the microsite and Facebook, Instagram, and Twitter while offering lucky fans exclusive rewards too. During the campaign, Coca-Cola sourced exceptional photos from the fans, including tear-jerking content of newlyweds enjoying Coca-Cola on their honeymoon. Several images were deemed shareable and narrated an emotional story of people which positively impacted the Coca-Cola brand.

6 Live in the moment

There's quite a stockpile of visual and video content for the consumption of buyers. There is also quite an opportunity for real-time engagement and interaction. When Benefit announced Kate Grant, an Irish model with Down's Syndrome, as their official model, the brand reminded many just how easy it is to be inclusive and promote customer engagement. Since the announcement, the company witnessed a great spike in engagement and sales. While this is not affirming that Benefit Cosmetics hired the model for selfish reasons, it is a worthy example of game-changing moves that companies can make to reach targets. Developing a robust video and image library filled with shareable content gives the company an edge to consistently add value. The opportunities and challenges are methods to determine the needed content. When you live in the moment, you also extend the content your brand needs. From traditional and wacky holidays to news of the day, and viral memes, there are no caps on the number of topics you can play with. But remember to stick to the company's values and leverage your strengths. And you do not want to look like you are taking advantage of a tragic event for marketing reasons. For instance, the Boston Marathon bombing tragedy in 2013 caught the attention of the world. Ford Motor Company's Scott

Monty, the head of global social media, tweeted to social media managers that it would be a good time to suspend more posts in honor of the bombing.

The companies who adhered to Monty's advice and posted heartfelt messages were adequately rewarded, while those who took advantage of the bombing to market their goods lost an excellent following and were dealt a blow to their reputation. A blizzard in Boston in 2013 also highlighted why you need to be timely and less promotional. As people were stuck in their homes, popular sports teams, the Boston Red Sox and the New England Patriots, revised their content calendars to focus on people's tweets, especially on the snowstorm. Wally the Green Monster, the Boston Red Sox's mascot buried waist-down in the snow at Fenway Park and the New England Patriots' parade of snowmen fan photos clad in their team gear showed how you could stay relevant without being promotional.

CHAPTER 4

VIDEO ENGAGEMENT

A CASE STUDY OF ZAPPOS

Zappos, the successful online retailer, has a reputation for mesmerizing its fan base with outstanding customer service, courtesy of the exceptional leadership of Tony Hsieh, Zappos' Chief Executive Officer. The company figured out early on that customers always have a tough time purchasing clothing and shoes on the internet. The primary cause, however, was that customers still had a hard time checking the fit of the purchase, which eventually determines if the item will be bought. And we all know how difficult it is to test fit from technical specifications.

Furthermore, Zappos observed that in-house customers would always make an emotional connection with preferred items—shoes or clothing—before purchase. Consumers always try to imagine how a purchase will make them feel and look. Will the chosen shoes make a nice pair with the prom dress? Will the suit impact confidence when I walk into the interview room?

Eventually, Zappos came up with a solution. They knew that the only way to bridge the gap between the brand and customers was to offer staff testimonials and personal advice—similar to what you'll get if you walk into a physical store and ask the staff for recommendations—to improve customer experience. Since its inception, they have more than 200,000 product videos to show for it. As more videos come up, customers get real-time information about products, and their expectations grow for that item. This is a winning strategy because videos have, for long, proven to establish a reliable connection between customer and brand, while creating trust too.

Videos for marketing

A company with enough time, skills, and capital can hire video marketers to make a high-quality video. Usually, this move certifies the brand as a legitimate company with genuine concerns for the customers, both prospective and existing. Because every social media channel has a different approach to storytelling, the metrics below, according to Global Uploads, in Q1 of 2015 highlight the top 1,000 by views for each platform:

Platform	Views per Video	Avg. Engagement	Avg. Video Length	Videos to reach 1M views in a month	Top Genre / Topic
Facebook	24 millio n	3.0%	1 min 28 seconds	694	Shocking or heartwarm ing
Instagram	1 millio n	430k per video	15 second s, max.	N/A	Pop culture
YouTube	17 millio n	0.65 %	12 minut es	271	Music

73 percent of businesses attest that videos are the most effective tool in marketing strategies. However, some useful

tips to keep in mind during the adoption of video marketing in any of your campaigns include:

- Make it short and concise; you must deliver the message in 1 minute or less

- The video ads must be strategically shared to be found with ease by the consumers

- There is a higher ROI when the video ad campaigns run regularly and consistently

- Make the video consumer-targeted for desktops and mobile-friendly, i.e. tablets and smartphones

Marketing videos can be about anything, but the goal remains the same— increase credibility, acquire views and viewers, and convert prospective customers.

Numbers by platform in 2015

Facebook	The new video formats on Facebook makes it quite competitive, as it garners more minutes of watch on YouTube. With more than 1 billion daily views on Facebook, about 65 percent come from mobile users.
Snapchat	The daily views on Snapchat total billions. Acquiring more than 4 billion views daily, it is expected that the current 1 percent of marketers who use Snapchat will increase with time.
Twitter	Twitter videos have improved one-on-one branding and listening. Videos uploaded on Twitter are majorly for social, direct, and real engagement.
YouTube	YouTube witnesses a daily upload of more than 300 hours of videos and puts the channel on top of the best marketing channels list.

No matter the choice of platform, do not forget that 'brevity' is an essential attribute of online videos. Indeed, you will find out that many consumers prefer videos that aren't more than 1 minute in length. Uploading short videos will keep the viewers interested in your product or service. Since there is tons of content available on the internet, you will expect a user to have a short attention span for your video.

Quality trumps quantity

Quality videos are sources of great information. But with small online businesses, the goal is to convey messages in an engaging, entertaining, and emotional format, without missing authenticity and accuracy. When you allow people to share and comment on your post and sometimes leave feedback, whether positive or negative, you improve the reputation of your business.

Negative feedback serves as a template to conduct better practices in your business to meet customers' expectations. And when you get such feedback, respond positively by trying to offer possible solutions to the problem. When other viewers see your mannerism and approach to negative feedback, they might feel inclined to purchase from you, as you have displayed trust and professionalism. Since video marketing is dynamic, feedback also helps the business improve video marketing strategies and campaigns to align with the target audience's needs. You must always analyze and alter the content of the video to achieve your goals. Constantly changing videos keeps the content relevant and exciting. For instance, you may make a series of videos about a topic, so that your viewers are always excited about new releases.

Making sure your audience finds your video

Search engine optimization is a method of optimizing your video to increase the possibility of listing your video on Google search engine by more than 50 percent. Indeed, when you combine videos with search engine optimization tools, you will enjoy many benefits and improve your business sporadically.

First, you must learn to use targeted keywords combined with more advanced SEO techniques in the construction of your video, since the action will place the video in the first search pages. Some studies show that many business owners use SEO techniques to promote their online content on Bing and Google. The same research shows that the first results page or top 10 results pages have the highest CTR. Therefore, incorporating SEO techniques with video marketing will also improve the search engine rankings of the company website.

With videos, you can expect the same. Usually, viewers are prompted to click on videos on a search engine results page, even if it is the 4th or 5th item after the 1st to 3rd written results.

Maximizing the power of SEO requires you to tag, name, and identify videos appropriately.

Another method of incorporating SEO techniques in videos is to provide an avenue for followers to like, share, and leave feedback. As stated earlier, feedback fuels views.

Other important SEO hacks:

❖ Upload the video with relevant text

❖ Create text transcripts of the video by increasing the use of keywords

❖ Marketing a video on the web

Good marketing reflects in the conversion rates. When you employ good marketing strategy, you increase the chances of getting more shares and views on your video. More so, if you feature a clickable link to your website, the likelihood that your customers will view your site is high. Social media channels are the most famous avenue for making videos accessible. A single video goes viral when thousands of viewers share the same video within their circle. This is the reason why video marketing is useful for traffic generation for both the product and the brand itself. The truth is that video marketing requires time and effort. For that reason, you can deploy video marketing services to promote viewership and interest. Since many online users are engaging different content at different times, you have to track the progress of your videos across the platforms and make significant changes. It's not news that some platforms work better for specific videos than others. Thus, it is essential to figure out which platform works best for your marketing campaign. It is a fact that video marketing boosts customer loyalty, increases sales, and promotes brand recognition. But the first step is to create video content and implement search engine optimization techniques. The second step is to distribute the video, strategically, on the internet. On completion of these steps, brands should see positive changes and improvements in operations.

CHAPTER 5

THE DISTRIBUTION OF
MARKETING VIDEOS

The popular reason why video marketing proves itself as a cheap way to promote business operations is because of the ready availability of video-sharing platforms. Such platforms, as we know, have been rated highly by search engines and their relevance rating is also the same. Thus, the creation of high-quality marketing videos and effective distribution via recommended channels is a sure way to promote business growth. For instance, a wind turbine business can create entertaining and informative content about wind farming and share such videos on a sharing site that is passionate about green energy. These video sharing websites are ultimately useful to boost brand recognition by targeting a broad and concentrated audience. Therefore, you have to consider relevant sites that will likely promote your business. Uploading these videos online may be tricky, technical, and time-consuming. As such, it is worth considering an agency that deals with marketing videos.

Video marketing agencies

Agencies that specialize in video marketing have surfaced over the years. And their distinct expertise on the subject matter becomes necessary because of the intricacy of business promotion. You should know that video marketing is often challenging if you don't have a full grasp of the concept or are unaware of current trends in business.

Another guarantee for success in your online business is in understanding the best method to incorporate standard customer engagement. Thus, your best bet is hiring the most suitable digital marketing agency. Working with a qualified digital marketing agency has more benefits than choosing traditional advertising companies.

Why?

- Digital marketing agencies have in-depth knowledge of the landscape, such as online broadcast, social media platforms, and online research tools and technology.

- Their expertise in determining the specific video content and concept for your business is unmatched.

- Vast knowledge of insightful and engaging themes and what resonates with your potential market.

- Certified digital marketing agencies can create quality and professional adverts that truly sell.

Using video marketing

There are several ways to gain recognition amongst your potential customer base and convert these people to actual buyers by using video marketing option. Depending on the specific message the business conveys, many videos can be adopted. Some of the ways online businesses can market their products have been mentioned before, but for the sake of reiteration, here is a comprehensive list:

Viral videos

You have probably heard or seen viral videos on your smartphones before now—from the famous 'Will it Blend?" series to Grumpy Cat, the list is endless. Most marketers post videos with the aim of going viral, but not everyone truly hits the mark. Before you invest your time and capital, understand that there is no precise formula to make your video go viral, and many successful viral campaigns happened by accident. However, you can try to increase the shareability of your video content.

What to look out for in video marketing

Before getting started, here are some tips for setting you on the right path. We know that many video styles are out there, but the most important thing is to find out what works for your business needs. Once you find the most suitable method, you can include other essential elements to videos—a call to action (CTA).

Tips to remember:

- ❖ Offer value to your target audience—both potential and returning customers

- ❖ Communicate a call to action—do you want them to subscribe to your service, make a purchase, share your video, or visit your company website?

The process of creating and distributing the video

Pre-production phase:

- ❖ Create a shooting script or storyboard

- ❖ Rehearse with your interview subjects or designated presenters

- ❖ Factor in possible additional footage

- ❖ Examine the logistics and acoustics of the filming location

- ❖ Shoot several takes of each scene

Post-production phase:

- ❖ Tidy up clips before assembling rough cuts, then

work out timing issues

❖ Don't abuse your video with many effects and transitions

❖ Verify your chosen music for any possible infringement on copyrights

Distribution phase:

These professional services can be considered for video distribution:

❖ PR Newswire – With hundreds of thousands of blogger contacts, journalists, and influencers, PR Newswire offers safe and secure distribution of video to an extensive media database

❖ Slide share – You can upload and share YouTube videos. Also, collect business leads and view count of your presentation as you do so

❖ Brightcove – The cloud content service provider offers a video platform for adding custom video players to mobile destinations, social media profiles, and video players

CONCLUSION

Video marketing is a necessary form of communication. And the continuous proliferation of online distribution platforms will bring about an increase in the use of such media platforms for business growth. Regardless of the size of your business, using videos is a worthy investment. Videos engage the customer base and differentiate the business from others. They also serve as a great medium to narrate company story, put the 'brand' in your business, and build trust with your customer base. Once you combine video creation and technology, you will efficiently and successfully compete within your niche.

Essential factors to consider for successful video marketing strategy

- ❖ Recognize your target audience and craft your message accordingly
- ❖ Plan, plan, plan
- ❖ Creativity fuels views, not a huge budget
- ❖ Execute, excellently
- ❖ Find the right distribution strategy to reach your goals

These strategies and more can help you leverage your video marketing campaign for continuity and sustainability.

When it comes to hiring a professional video marketer, research isn't enough, which is why I am offering free consultations to business owners who want a professional to create enticing videos. Click the link here to set up an appointment today so we can elevate your business to a new level.